FROM THE PORCH

Gentle and humorous reflections of life
on a small island off the North Coast of Florida

by Dickie Anderson

Cover Photos by Andy Strait. Copyright 2002.

Hardcover:
ISBN 0-9716081-2-1
First Edition
First Printing

Library of Congress Control Number: 2002093636

1. Southern Regional 2. Humor 3. Lifestyle 4. Columnist

To Order:
Author To Author Promotions
17 Williams Street
St. Augustine, FL 32084
(904) 826-0454
www.author2author.com
author2author@hotmail.com

Published by:
Market Maker
(904) 261-2425
dickiemm@bellsouth.net
www.dickieanderson.com

"She is both knowledgeable and charmingly entertaining – in other words – a natural"

~Carol Ann Atwood, Amelia Island Museum of History

"Like her signature straw hat, Dickie Anderson's observations sparkle with romantic ideals and stern practicality and her porch is the coolest spot around"

~Joani Selement, Book Island Festival, Amelia Island, Florida

"Dickie Anderson has IT! …Her ability to take everyday events and turn them into something that frequently leaves you laughing or, at the very least, smiling, is a rare talent and one which Dickie has in abundance"

~Kay Braverman
Iowa City, Iowa

"She sees humor and beauty in the everyday... focusing on family, friendship and community"

~Anne Chasser
Washington DC

"She's Amelia's answer to Charles Kuralt"
~Jan Davis

Dedicated to my number one cheerleader,
my love, my husband Shelly.

CONTENTS

SPRING

SUMMER

FALL

WINTER

Introduction

From The Porch? Yes, the stories, actually columns, are based on marshside musings as I sip a cool drink and relax on my backyard porch.

For six years, Amelia Island has been my home. My love affair with the thirteen-mile long island that nestles in the most northeastern corner of Florida is clear to those who read my weekly column.

I would like to thank the *Florida Times-Union* for giving me the opportunity to find my voice. For two years, my weekly columns, From The Porch, have shared stories about the gentle, sometimes amusing life in my beloved Mayberry By The Sea. Thanks, to all who encourage me everyday and are the inspiration for my writing.

Now, come join me on the porch.

Dickie

www.dickieanderson.com

Reprinted by permission of:
Nassau Neighbors, *The Florida Times-Union*, Amelia Island, Florida
Special thanks to Susan Respess, Derek Kinner and Larry Boatwright.

SPRING

Garden of Eden?

It is an addiction. The call to the garden. My dogs join me for a casual early morning stroll around the yard with my morning cup of coffee. More often than not, I see things that need attention. Each sad little clump seems to call me. "Trim me, spray me, water me," and sometimes "Bury me." After a spell of cool weather, there is major repair and removal work to be done. We are cautioned not to jump the gun. Any cutting will initiate growth that may create damage if the temperatures play more games with us.

We transplants (interesting choice of words) particularly enjoy the wonderful variety of plants and flowers that grow in our new home and don't miss the bare trees and colorless landscape we left behind. It made me grin when I spotted the tall tassel topped palm in my new home's back yard – the ultimate tropical icon.

As spring approaches, it is time for spring housecleaning or garden cleaning. First, an inventory of existing plants. Some brave and colorful flowers have stayed the winter and are a pleasant surprise; pansies with their silly faces and the incredible ever-patient impatients.

The first warm days of spring bring a frenzy of outdoor activity. Like a land rush gardeners will scurry to the local discount stores and garden centers to buy, buy, buy and plant, plant, plant. I should have a bumper sticker that proclaims "I Break For Flowers"!

I find myself, particularly in the spring, stopping at every discount store and garden center breaking for flowers as I inspect the flats of brilliantly colored bedding plants. Instead of sneaking in the house with shopping bags from the mall, spring finds me sneaking yet another flat of petunias, marigold, salvia, and zinnia – as my husband looks on in disbelief. "Never too many flowers," I cheerfully state, as I head outside to settle my new purchases in my marsh side yard.

Driving around the island forces us to pass the beautifully manicured lawns and gardens of our local hotels and resorts. On a daily basis, armies of earnest workers are bent at their task of pulling up perfectly healthy happy plants and replacing them with the flavor of the month. It brings to mind the chaos in *Alice in Wonderland,* as the Queen of Hearts demands that her roses be painted red. In a blink of the eye, red and white petunias are changed to blankets of purple pansies tucked around the artfully manicured bushes and trees.

We all have favorites. I have always favored, the user-friendly day lilies – many colors and forms and forgiving of bad soil, random watering and excessive temperatures. They only beg to be pinched to keep their blossoms coming. Geraniums are also wonderfully forgiving of neglect and continue to bloom through thick and thin, ranging from orange red to pale pink to white, and I am a sucker for the cliché hibiscus with exotic blossoms begging to be tucked behind an ear.

A day spent digging in the dirt with birds singing in the trees, a cool breeze and the freshest of air pulling at my hair is a priceless gift. Full of yard work exhaustion, I melt into my comfortable porch chair, savor the sunset and enjoy the fruits (or flowers) of my labors.

Battle For The Garden

We enjoy the warm air and the lush, tropical flowers and plants around us, but with these gifts come a price. Where beautiful hibiscus, oleander and bougainvillea grow, so do other living, growing things — some, clearly, designed by the devil himself. With all the beauty of spring and our return to our gardens come the munching, crunching biting insects and invasive weeds, challenging us at every turn.

I feel a certain level of envy as armies of earnest workers in matching shirts pull into our neighbors' driveways in trucks full to the brim with mowers and tools of all kinds. In a blink, they are gone and the yard is "done". Like a trip to the beauty parlor – the once unkempt, shaggy lawn is newly clipped and coifed.

Not at our house - with my husband it is a point of pride. We can do it ourselves. We cannot only do it better, but save lots of money. So we fight the weeds and pests and sometimes nearly kill ourselves in the heat, bleeding from palmetto cuts and scratching at ant bites. We fight the good fight.

There are many trips to our local garden center and consultations with the resident "pharmacist" result in a shopping bag full of powders, sprays and granules. Each promises a perfect cure and we are eager to test their claims and have a yard that looks like the colorful photos on the packaging.

My husband focuses on the evil dollar weed. Clearly it loves our climate and in particular our little piece of ground. It spreads across our lawn like miniature water lilies. In his passion for battle, he once sprayed the spreading dollar weed with the specified potion and not satisfied that it was working he attacked once again. This time it did work – so well, that we had an Agent Orange effect for weeks. Balance returned and it all finally grew out like a bad haircut.

My specialty is the grabbing grasping grapevines that defy imagination in their unlimitless ability to grow everywhere over everything. When I go on a vine rampage I am a woman possessed - unstoppable – pulling and piling the vines as I go. Free at last, the plants released from the bondage of the grasping vines almost seem to stretch to enjoy their new freedom and the sunny day.

Perhaps the most bizarre and painful enemy of the backyard gardener is the dreaded red ant whose armies build their little mounds in the most strange and frustrating places - at the base of a mailbox, in my favorite day lily garden, near the entrance to the back door to my garage. We respond with boiling water or prepackaged granules of poison designed to kill the queen and force retreat. As pesky and irritating as these little warriors are, you have to admire their stone-headed determination as they reorganize to build another castle for their queen!

It is not all work – working side by side, my husband and I enjoy the exhaustion of a day in the yard and a certain amount of back patting as we settle on the porch at the end of the day.

For The Birds

I guess you could say we're for the birds. We truly enjoy the entertainment they provide and are more then happy to keep our feeders full. We brought our enjoyment of feeding birds from our Mid-Western roots, where birds truly depend on the generosity of those who put out food and water in the challenging cold of deep winter. We are now treated to the delights of many colorful birds that make our warmer climes their home.

There are cat people, there are dog people and there are bird people. It is not mutually exclusive, but the mix of cats and birds is not always a good one. Sometimes cat owners who have house bound cats buy bird feeders to entertain their captive pets. Dogs rarely bother yard birds, but those bred for hunting can pull a grown man down a beach at a very rapid pace when the turkey-sized gulls take flight.

Spring is a busy time for our year round bird populations and we enjoy the migrating visitors that stop for a few days or weeks and move on. Part of living in a warmer climate is the delightful potpourri of birds that abound along the coasts of Florida and Georgia.

Birds, like people, may affect a variety of color options in the appearance. Goldfinches crowd our thistle feeders in the early spring. The brilliant yellow of these feisty little birds is a treat to the eye. Of course, the regal crimson Cardinals are regulars and stop often reminding us of our feeders hung from snowy trees so many years ago. The Blue Jays, bossy and loud, make regular stops. The Red-winged Black Birds come in like a gang on motorcycles; their shiny black feathers set off with epaulets of bright red and, at certain times of the year, yellow. They are a noisy gang and demanding if the seed is low in their favorite feeder.

My favorite? No contest. The Mona Lisa of all birds is the Painted Bunting, which does indeed look painted. Once you see them, you will never forget the male with its incredible combination of blue, red and green. Of course, the male is the flashiest, but the gentle female is beautiful in her own way. She is delicate of profile and is an almost iridescent greenish yellow. Locals call these colorful visitors the tax birds as they often appear on April 15.

Our porch overlooks a tidal marsh, which resembles a busy airport at the end of each day. We see a wide variety of flight patterns as the bigger birds come to feed or rest for the night. They wade in the marsh looking for things to eat. Egrets, Herons and Woodstorks display their flying agility and are "oh so" elegant as they fly like ballerinas with wings and slowly circle down. Then they land. Marsh landings are mostly graceful, but if you have ever watched a Heron or Stork try to land on a pine limb it rivals the best of any circus clown balancing act you have ever seen.

Our porch at the end of the day provides us a quiet place to watch the birds as they come in shifts and find our feeders. They love the sprinkler system that comes on at the end of the day and flit in and out entertaining us. Such simple pleasures and no commercials!

Hooked

Mother-son fishing? Is that an oxymoron? A contradiction? At least to me, it was a very special day shared with my son. When the telephone rang and my son announced a business trip bringing him to our Northern Florida home, I was thrilled. Just before he hung up he suggested that we might go fishing. The telephone safely in its cradle, I reflected, smiled and thought back over the years.

I have always dubbed my middle son my "yup/nope" son, always a boy of few words and single focus. One focus, his passion for fishing, has lasted from early childhood. Passion may even be an understatement.

As a youngster, his favored times were those fishing in the ponds, lakes and rivers of Iowa. Now grown and launched in a career his driving passion remains fishing. It has punctuated his life as he grew up, graduated from college and began his career.

My fishing companion arrived on a Friday and early the next morning, we stumbled around in the darkness pulling on our clothes and gathering some basic supplies. We arrived at the dock in the darkness of pre-dawn and found the only sign of life a rather scruffy group of pelicans silently standing watch. Shortly after our arrival, our guide pulled up, greeted us and backed our craft for the day down the launch ramp.

We watched the sleek, white, immaculate fishing boat ease into the dark lapping water. The boat leveled and began to bob gently. We climbed in and set off on our early morning adventure. As the rosy early morning light began to fill the sky, the three - mother, boy and guide left the Fernandina Beach Harbor behind us. We looked back as the sun's bright morning light silhouetted the sleepy town. Our adventure had begun.

We headed out into the Intracoastal Waterway to explore the marshes and islands around Amelia Island. We were "hunting" red fish, a spirited fish offering sport to fisherman and eating pleasure to the seafood connoisseur. As the tide retreats, the red fish head into the shallows to round up the smaller fish that they feed on.

Our guide stood on a small platform at the boat's rear and searched the shallows for "tailing" red fish. Soon swirling water flagged red fish feeding and we quickly began to cast our colorful lures as close to the breaking water as we could. Slowly we cast and reeled in the lures through the dark water. As we continued to cast and reel in, cast and reel in – the sun continued to rise.

My first efforts were somewhat frantic, but I soon settled into a rhythm. Then BANG - instant attention as a rod tip bent. Our guide had hooked a red! He passed the rod to me, smiled and instructed me to slowly bring the fish in - the fish would run, but hunkering in, I continued to keep tension on my line and bring in my fish. When the fish chose to run I let him run. My adrenaline pumped as the rod arched and released, arched and released as the fish pulled. The water was only a few feet deep and the big fish ran pulling at the line. His tail broke water as he fought to escape. As instructed, I let him run and then slowly reeled him in. The fish began to tire, but as he got closer to the boat, he began a new struggle, which included a side trip not only under but also all around the boat. A square dance ensued as my son and the guide struggled to get out of the way, as they encouraged my efforts.

The fish was finally close enough to be netted. I stared in wonder at this beautiful, not-at-all red, but rather silvery fish, that I had pulled out of marsh waters. It was decreed twenty-two inches and six plus pounds - in other words a "keeper" - above the legal limit.

We settled back into our fishing rhythm and soon we hooked another red. This fish, smaller in size, we did release. The guide and I sat back as my son, attracted to the pure sport and art of fly-fishing selected a fly rod and moved to the front of the boat. We settled down to watch the graceful snap of the fly rod as he dropped the fly near the swirling water, which marked the feeding ground of the red fish. We watched as he, with deep concentration, repeated the graceful motion dropping the fly near the feeding fish, letting the colorful floating fish line settle on the surface of the marsh waters and then the slow process of pulling in the line by hand hoping for a "hit". His technique was perfect and I could see the guide's silent approval as we watched the intense young man's determined efforts to tempt a red fish to take the fly. Several fish made a pass, but did not take the fly, so we moved on.

The sun high in the sky signaled it was time to head back. We settled down for the ride home enjoying the beauty of the Intracoastal Waterway - to the Fernandina Beach marina where we had started out so many hours ago.

A framed photograph of a beaming mother, tall son and gleaming fish held well forward to emphasize its size, now reminds me of our delightful outing on a beautiful, sunny, spring morning off the coast of North Florida's marshlands.

Call To Cumberland

Cumberland Island, the most southern barrier island off the coast of Georgia, is one of my favorite places to share. Visible from the north end of Amelia Island, Cumberland Island is a National Park and allows only limited access. The island has much to share - its wild, unspoiled natural beauty and its amazing history. On a beautiful sunny day, full of promise, my younger sister, visiting here from Boston, joined me to discover for herself what was so magical about this island. Her adventures have taken her around the world and it is no small task to impress her.

One sunny Florida morning we boarded the Miss Lucy and left the dock at Fernandina Beach with a small group of fellow travelers. We looked back at the little town's familiar and almost timeless skyline. Our 45-minute boat ride took us north crossing the St. Mary's River, which separates Amelia Island and Cumberland Island.

Approaching Cumberland Island, we continued along the western edge passing several private docks and finally pulling up at the Greyfield Inn dock. The Greyfield Inn, now an elegant bed and breakfast, was the summer cottage to one of the many Carnegie family members that lived a charmed life so many years ago. We scrambled out of the boat and headed up to the inn with its umbrella of towering, twisted live oaks and wide welcoming porch.

A young man welcomed us and gave us a brief orientation. The inn, proud of its shabby chic reputation, welcomes its guests and invites them to help themselves and make themselves at home. The inn offers a cozy living room with books, natural treasures found on the beaches and forests of the island and pictures of family members from years past, who somehow do not seem to mind sharing their special place. We picked up our picnic lunches from the large and friendly kitchen in the lower level of the inn and headed out to the big white barn to select our bicycles.

Lunches tucked in our backpacks and eager to begin our adventure we mounted our big-tire bicycles and headed out along the sandy road toward the ruins of Dungeness, a Carnegie mansion, on the south end of the island. First timers are always charmed by the tunnel of live oaks and the dense palmetto growth along the dusty road - the road appears to go forever and it feels like forever for those not used to bicycles or the uneven sandy road bed.

We soon came to the gate leading to the ruins of the once elegant and now crumbling Dungeness mansion. Elements of the house still stand and have a regal charm even in decay. As we walked around the grounds, we marveled at the wilderness around us and tried to imagine the elegant gardens and charmed life lived so many years ago.

Our next stop - the glorious beach with its snowy white, fine-grained sand that stretches to the horizon. The day we visited, we were lucky enough to see horses along the edge of the sea, their tails blowing in the gentle wind.

The beach offered an ideal place to enjoy our picnic. Ducking out of the wind, we unpacked our lunches and settled back to watch the sea birds ride the currents of air above us. One particular brave gull landed five feet away, stood determinedly staring at us, and watched as we ate our lunches. We stood firm and did not encourage the begging by indulging our determined, uninvited luncheon guest.

Leaving the beach we headed back to the Greyfield Inn, retracing our steps as we pedaled along the sun dappled road that led us back to the inn. We climbed the front stairs and settled on the large inviting porch swing at the far end of the building. We relaxed into the peace and quiet that is so much a part of the Cumberland experience. As we gently swayed back and forth, it seemed like time had stopped, if only for a moment. But, of course, time doesn't stop and we soon answered the call to catch the boat home.

It's OK, though, I know Cumberland is there and I will return. And, yes, I have another convert. My sister agrees Cumberland Island is right up there on the list of unique and special places in the world.

Confessions of a Street Walker

My day starts with a morning walk. I try to make it a part of my daily routine and truly savor the time with my husband and two small dogs. It is more than the exercise we both know we need. It is a piece of time that is precious to us. We walk out of the house, leaving our busy lives behind and take the time to enjoy the beauty of the island and truly catch up with what is going on in our lives. Our talk can be of politics, our busy children, our schedule for the day, the grocery list or some major decision we are mulling over. Uninterrupted by phone or television we are actually able to finish complete sentences.

Our two Yorkshire Terriers count on this daily outing and trot down the street leading the way. We meet other walkers sometimes with dogs and sometimes not. We pass and greet single, determined walkers or pairs of friends enjoying the morning and shared exercise. We pass Bob and his borrowed dog jogging at a steady pace. We pass an older gentleman that is being more walked by his leash-pulling dogs than vice versa. We worry for his safety.

As we walk, we pass a gallery of dogs, all sizes and dispositions, all looking at us and wagging their tails in greeting, but not straying from their yard. We are a neighborhood of invisible fences and the well-mannered group that greets us each morning is testimony to their effectiveness. My small dogs gloat a bit as we progress down the road. They strut, all six pounds each, with the full-blown confidence of one on the outside as they pass each captive.

Our walks are not all pleasure. There is considerable work to be done. We inspect all houses under construction and take our responsibility as unofficial construction-observation-supervisors very seriously. We have walked through most of the homes under construction in our neighborhood in the last few years. We wander through the chaos of an unfinished house and try to figure out which room is which and ponder the views from each of the windows taking shape. We watch with curiosity as progress is made and then as completion approaches the final frosting on the cake - green frosting - new sod in carpet-like squares. Weeks later it is difficult to remember the skeleton of the first raw framing so many months ago.

Another morning walk activity is trash detail. We pick up trash along the way. Usually it is fast food wrappers and cups. What an interesting and unusual marketing survey we can make by inspecting the daily road trash - you can tell what the most popular or most convenient fast food options are. More often than not, the litter is beer cans left by the construction workers as they leave to go home. Instead of the trail of crumbs left by Hansel and Gretel, the trail out of our neighborhood is that of beer cans.

Our walks are a treasured part of our daily schedule. It is a good way to start the day.

Empty House Warming

A beautiful "old lady" on South Seventh Street in the Historic District of Fernandina Beach has come alive. Located in Fernandina Beach's historic district, you will find her sitting primly next to a much larger and grander house. The grand house is a rambling Victorian home known in the district as the Waas House, for the family who built it and lived in it. The smaller house is known as Grandma Waas' house, a Victorian cottage, built for the family's grandmother. Like so many of the Victorian homes in Fernandina Beach, this house, with only four owners, has remained relatively unspoiled by earnest, but destructive remodeling.

In the spring of 2001, the sleepy lady got new owners. The circa-1890 house was offered for sale and a brave couple, world travelers and con-noisseurs of history and architecture, immediately saw the possibilities of the sleeping beauty on South Seventh Street. The couple stepped up to join the select club of passionate restorers of Fernandina Beach's painted ladies; the Victorian houses built in the late 1800s.

From The Porch

The house has an intricate white wooden fence along the sidewalk. A gate opens to a brick path that leads to the welcoming house-wide front porch. The wooden front door shows off some long-forgotten craftsman's carpentry skills with inserts of stained glass and an irresistible old brass bell inviting people inside.

Thrilled to have secured their cottage in the historic district, the couple hosted a party before they moved in - "an empty house warming" to celebrate the re-awaking of the little cottage. As if they knew something was afoot, days before the party, tangled plantings around the house showed signs of life. There were azaleas, pale pink camellias just opening and lush green ferns unfolding from a winter's sleep. Even the jonquils had popped up along the front fence.

Friends helped transform the house into a party site that afternoon, darting from room to brightly colored room, filling each with the bright spring flowers, cut and picked from the gardens surrounding the house. Old family silver, freshly polished, gleamed. Yards of lacy fabric were draped around the house to "disguise" mystery doors or things better left unseen.

Another team worked on the food - washing strawberries and dipping them in chocolate, chopping hardboiled eggs and toasting bread for the caviar that would top them. Dishes brimmed with truffles and other chocolate delicacies. The cozy buzz of women working in the kitchen filled the house. The men tended to guy stuff, insuring that the sound system functioned, the outside lighting worked, a new lock was installed on the powder room door and that the back deck with its tiered iron fountain was power-washed.

The guests arrived in the evening, dressed up for fun, in tuxedos, long dresses, furs and jewels. Champagne toasts were made to the old owner and the new. All agreed Grandma Waas must have been smiling as the gathering showed that the old house still enjoyed a good party.

Two Weeks in Provence – On A Bicycle

Adventure travel stories fill magazines and newspapers and for good reason. Biking, walking, barging - whatever your mode du jour, it is an amazing way to see a country, feel its essence and enjoy its beauty at the most basic level. Travel is a shake up. My husband and I made the leap and set off on a two-week adventure that would take us to southern France and fabled Provence and we did it on bicycles. We like our exercise. The combination of the physical challenge and seeing a new and exciting part of the world seemed a perfect match.

We planned and dreamed about our trip for many months and trained as best we could on the flat roads of northern Florida. We carefully selected our clothing, as we were limited to a duffel bag and a backpack. A van would transport our luggage from stop to stop and we would travel by bicycle.

Yes, there would be challenges. The time change, for us six hours, is part of the adventure. You just handle it, like taking a bitter tonic. Some are blessed with an easy tolerance to hours lost or gained and some are not. Our experience was not too bad as we laid over in Paris for one day then took a gentle train ride to Avignon in southern France to meet our group.

Every challenge - using different money, trying to ask directions, finding things and places may add a certain tension, but the golden moments are worth every little frustration and unpleasant surprise. You successfully order something in a different language, you find a small souvenir; crude and charming, you see views that fill the eye with images that are somehow different from any that you have ever seen.

Our destination met our every expectation. Provence has become more then a geographic region; it is a way of life. There is a kind of wonderful white light that warms its gentle and sometimes daunting hills and sweeping valleys. Each little town held its own special charm - bright shutters, flowers and plants of every sort and kind and always the French dogs. No one will argue. Dogs rule and are welcome everywhere including hotels and restaurants.

We were rewarded repeatedly, as we explored Provence with our 18 fellow bicycle adventurers. Each day brought special travel moments. We rode through the countryside, eating at sidewalk cafés, tasting new things and watching the pace and pattern of a different people and settings that charmed us with their color, energy and beauty.

Part of the joy of travel is the forced changed of pattern in our lives. We learned to eat later at night and take our time savoring our meals and our conversation with other people in our group. We learned to use Euros and speak our own language of French-English and sometimes a little Spanish.

Travel is life changing - and I do not mean we came home fatter and poorer, but we came home with a broader vision and enjoyment of our own time and place.

The Good Old Days

Recently, while spending time with my father, I spent some time sorting through an old trunk containing bits and pieces of our family history. One particular dusty box found in the trunk contained memorabilia from my mother's side of the family.

Mother's side of the family is a curiosity, as she was an only child of two only children and there is no one left to answer the questions never asked so long ago. The box I held in my hand was a window into the past.

There was much to learn as I read through dry, yellowed clippings carefully saved in albums by my grandmother and her mother. Details of weddings and funerals in such detail that you could see the bride, know the history of her dress and the lace handkerchief she carried. You knew who was at the reception and what kind of flowers were on the tables. The obituaries gave you wonderfully detailed histories of those that had died and, for me, filled in some empty slots in my mother's history.

Also in the old box were notes written over the years on beautiful stationery in graceful loopy handwriting thanking someone for an occasion or a gift or simply a congratulatory message. How many such notes do we receive today? Sadly, few.

I am afraid that social graces have been left in the dust of computers, communication by email, voice mail and cell phone. We are all in such a hurry to get places, to move information - efficiency is our goal, not graciousness. Yes, I am guilty. I carry a cell phone and use all the tools of rapid communication. My thank you notes are often by email or forgotten in my busy days. I sense both my well-mannered grandmothers chastising me for this thoughtlessness.

In a recent conversation with a friend, we recalled the social graces that were so much a part of our childhoods. Curtseys, bows, personal notes, hostess gifts, dressing for special occasions - rare today. We were taught to ask, "May I?" and always to say "Thank you." We may have grumbled as youngsters as we were reminded of our manners, but we knew what was expected of us. Many of us now miss the thoughtful respect that was part of those social graces, which we were taught as children.

I was able to capture just a bit of those golden, gentle days of social gentility on a beautiful Saturday afternoon in Washington, DC more than a year ago. The occasion? A shower for my daughter-in-law to be, then living in Washington, DC. Three generations of ladies gathered at the grand dowager of a landmark building in the nation's capital – the Mayflower Hotel.

From The Porch

The Mayflower celebrates the gentler times when people took time for afternoon tea and enjoyed each other's company in no great hurry to rush off to another appointment or event. No grabbing a latte at Starbucks. Tea at the Mayflower is served with all the ceremony of days gone by. As the shower guests arrived, escaping the noisy Washington traffic, they found a beautiful table elegantly set for afternoon tea. Waiters dressed in smart black and white began bringing lemon curd, clotted cream, tiers of elegant tea cookies arranged on individual silver trays, and of course, freshly brewed tea in individual pots.

Three generations gathered around the linen draped table. The youngest attending? The bride in her late twenties, dressed in spring bright pink, and her potpourri of high-energy friends. The young women were enchanted with the idea of individual teapots and freshly brewed tea and the lovely cookies and tarts. The middle generation, my generation, included the bride's mother and a close friend living in Washington who shared the hostessing duty. In our own way, we each recalled our wedding showers so long ago.

The oldest generation? Two long time friends of my mother, who had died a year before, both in their eighties, braved the city traffic. Each in their party clothes complete with pearls brought a very special blessing to the afternoon tea, and for me, an essence of my mother no longer with me.

Presents were opened, stories swapped and toasts were made to the bride-to-be. As each guest said their proper goodbyes, they remarked on how nice it was to take the time to sit over tea at the Mayflower and share time with three generations of women.

So maybe we can, at least for a time, recapture some of the of the lost social graces and share them with a new generation. We are challenged to bring back that extra effort and respect for others that makes us ladies and gentlemen.

From The Porch

SUMMER

Beach Yoga

I have a new habit. Unlike many of my others this is a good one. Three days a week I wake up and pull on a pair of shabby beach shorts and a T-shirt and head to the beach for my morning beach yoga class.

Sometimes groggy, I unfold my mat and spread my towel. I greet my fellow early morning yoga buddies and sit cross-legged, waiting for the teacher, to begin. Our teacher has recently moved to Amelia Island from Hawaii and offers beginning yoga classes. She herself is a living testimonial to the healing power of yoga. A bright, highly athletic girl, she actively participated in many activities in Hawaii, including cross-country running, surfing, tennis and bicycling.

She lived a dream life in a tropical paradise. Then the unthinkable happened. She suffered an anterior gas embolism while on a scuba dive. Her life was forever changed. She struggled with partial paralysis on one side, dyslexia and wondered if her self-confidence and love of life would return. It did. Her current confidence and success come from the discipline, strength and conditioning that yoga brought to her. If yoga was a critical part of her rehabilitation then I could only benefit.

OK, I'll admit it. When I first attended the beginning classes, I went because her mother is a good friend and I wanted to support this fledgling activity. I was also just plain curious. Would I be sitting around draped in a sheet, humming? Could I become thin and stress free? I had to give it a try. Yoga is not a religion or a sport, as our teacher reminds us. It is about our individual relationship with our lives and bodies. It is what we make it. Although we sit in a circle on the beach, we are alone in many ways.

Like children, we each unroll our straw mats and spread a towel on top. I find myself feeling a little like a child in day-care, with my very own mat, ready for naptime. We begin by sitting in a comfortable position and focusing on just letting go. We then proceed through a series of stretches and positions, each with a different effect. Some feel wonderful and some are difficult, but you know they're helping. As we relax into our hour of yoga, the world goes on around us. Briskly moving dog-walkers, joggers, and families with small children all pass the quiet circle on the beach.

Our teacher's confident voice is soothing as she leads us through the poses that are targeted at different parts of our bodies and types of stress. There is no impact or frantic waving of arms and legs. Each pose flows to the next.

We end by thanking each other for sharing the hour on the beautiful Amelia Island beach. Picking up our mats and dusting sand off our arms and legs, we set off to start our days with a sense of serenity, which we hope will carry us through the day.

If My Machine Talks to Your Machine, Are We Communicating?

What have we come to? No more person-to-person communication – now it is machine to machine. More often than not, I find I leave a message. When a real live person answers the phone I become tongue-tied. Sputtering, I attempt to recover and reorganize my thoughts. Remember the first days of voice mail?

In those early days, when I placed a call and found an answering machine asking for a message I would panic. Performance anxiety overwhelmed me. Hanging up, I would script my message and call back. Now leaving messages is an art. Many conversations are held without one real-person to real-person connection.

And haven't we all struggled with performance anxiety recording our own message to be heard on answering machines or voice mail? I admit it – I have tried over and over to get the perfect message – not too long, not too short. When I call my sister's machine, (note: not my sister but my sister's machine) I have so many options regarding where she might be reached that I forget why I called.

Picking up voice mail is always an adventure. I sometimes feel like I am playing a musical instrument as I utilize all the buttons to delete, skip or repeat the messages. Some of the messages are quick and to the point and some are long and newsy. Some of the longer messages are so conversational that I find myself responding to the recorded message.

And haven't we all been at the other end of a call, usually to a business, where all we want is to talk to a "real" person? So what do we get? Options – press one if you want to talk to the credit department, press two if you want to make a purchase, press three, etc. Somehow, the options do not even fit the parameters that we seek. My general approach is when in doubt press "0" – it often works, but not always. Sometimes it starts the whole menu again.

When I am not meeting the challenges of telephone communication, I am clicking away on my computer. OK, OK, I admit it, I am an email junkie – I love the instant communication with friends and family. Monday mornings I send a chatty group email to my children who are scattered along the East Coast. I am never able to reach them by phone and they would say the same of me, so email is our communication medium. As they respond they respond to all, so we each get instant and shared information.

What have we lost in all these current communication technologies? We have lost the joy of hearing the "real" voice of a loved one or old friend at the other end of the phone. So as we master the new communication technologies we need to remember the art of person to person communication by letter and voice. Someone once said to me you have to be smarter than your technology. It is getting harder and harder.

Call The Doctor, My Computer Has A Virus

Today's news is full of attacks of different kinds occurring around the world. My battles are closer to home. I am experiencing a formidable enemy - computer viruses. Not alone, I am fighting unwelcome and unexpected visitors to my computer.

You would think we were discussing a Yellow Fever epidemic instead of problems with our computers. Many of us have been attacked by aggressive computer viruses that have left our valued files contaminated and put into quarantine. We are even guilty of spreading the viruses to business associates, friends and family members.

My computer is a victim. It had a virus and files had to be quarantined - very personal. How can this be? Our own health depends on how well we take care of our bodies. Clearly, our computers need the same due diligence and preventive maintenance. I recently paid for my neglect and found myself seeking a specialist.

The first symptom? I lost all my photo files. I had amassed an amazing variety of family pictures, which included weddings, showers, vacations, celebrations, children, dogs, holidays, etc. In addition, I had retained many photos taken as a freelancer for *The Florida Times-Union*... all stored in my computer. The more I tried to figure out what was wrong the worse it got.

"Not good," one of my sons and the family computer whiz said, when I called to ask for his long-distance advice. "New hard drive," he said. Not the diagnosis I had hoped for.

When all else fails, call the doctor. I put a call into my local computer expert, AKA the Computer Doc. He listened patiently to my problems and suggested I bring the "tower" in and he would give it a thorough examination to see what was up.

I disconnected endless wires, hoping I would remember how to reconnect the red, yellow and green lifelines, and carried the ailing patient to my car. When I arrived, the doctor was in. The patient was put on the examining table. Several questions were asked concerning symptoms.

You know the feeling when you finally go to the dentist after going too long between cleanings? I looked at the floor and shuffled my feet. No, I had not updated my virus scan and no I did not back up my files. He smiled a gentle and patient smile and suggested I leave the computer for a more thorough examination and he would be in touch.

So I left the computer feeling strangely naked. My computer is my lifeline. It connects me to my children and my friends spread across the country. It makes airline reservations for me. It does my research for my writing. I am able to send my stories via computer and even the pictures that accompany the stories. It answers medical questions. It has 200 pages of a book in progress. It has been my photo album since my digital camera changed my photo-taking habits. It has a cup of coffee with me each morning. It is my first stop when I return from a trip. It keeps my calendar and it is my main address book. I was lost.

Later in the day, I checked with the computer clinic, crossing my fingers that there would be good news. The diagnosis? I had a "worm". A worm? Gosh, I heard of worming dogs and cats but never a computer. The files were cleaned, but my photos were lost forever. An on-line Anti-Virus program was recommended and installed. In addition, I now have a CD burner and will back-up files.

Released from treatment, the computer came home and to my amazement, I was able to reconnect the tangle of multi-colored wires needed to make it run. Now my friend, fit and healthy, is back in place. Ah, thank goodness for modern medicine.

The "Drawer"

I chuckled as I recently caught up with a friend who was going through a move. She had been doing the final cleaning of the house she had just sold. She was sure that it had been pretty well cleaned out. But, no. She found the "drawer". You know what is coming. We all have a drawer or possibly multiple drawers that defy organization and reveal a great deal about our lives. I have at least one in every room. Sometimes I move things from one drawer to another, but never, never throw anything away.

Where does all that stuff in our drawers come from and why can't we throw it away? I have to admit that I transfer things from my purse to one of my drawers. My purse is sort of a portable drawer. It contains many of the same useless things that I keep in the drawers and never seem able to throw away.

From The Porch

It occurs to me that these drawers are not unlike an archaeological dig. Not only do they have stuff in them that is very old, they have stuff in them that takes a well-trained scientist to identify. It is terrifying to contemplate what these drawers might reveal about us to future generations. Hundreds of years from now an archaeologist would quickly know that my husband played golf, we used suntan lotion and bug spray, we wore glasses to see, I wore Blossom Pink lipstick and was missing one gold earring. Old grocery lists would reveal our eating habits.

When the subject of "drawers'" came up at breakfast one morning, my husband and I began to reminisce about past drawers in our lives. The visions of past drawers consumed us and, throughout the day, we would call out to each other when yet another drawer candidate would come to mind. Out-dated football schedules he'd call. I'd respond Christmas ornament hooks and the tiny replacement bulbs for strings of lights. As our list grew it seemed to become gender sensitive.

His drawer might have: sunglasses, golf tees, nail clippers, match books long aged to the point of ineffectiveness, bad batteries, old score cards from long ago golf games, a screw driver, change, always change - endless pennies.

Her drawer might have: single earrings, old lipsticks (long worn down but a color you want to remember), not enough birthday cake candles for the cake you are trying to decorate, buttons from clothes that have long gone to charity, buttons in little tiny plastic bags pulled from new clothing, expired coupons and old grocery lists that never made it to the grocery store.

Future archaeologists would be able to detect the presence of children by sorting through the odds and ends found in a drawer. When my boys were younger our family drawer often included: expired lunch tickets, wrong length shoe laces for athletic shoes, lock combinations to long lost locks, or locks with no combinations - they never matched. There were incomplete decks of cards, odd game pieces, marbles, toys from fast food restaurants, Match Box cars and Weebles.

Then there are the keys. All drawers have mystery keys. You know, the keys that you are afraid to throw away and have no idea what they might open. Keys to what? It is almost as if a spell has been cast on these keys that prevents us from throwing them away. We have even been guilty of moving keys from state to state. Has anyone ever been able to match a key to a lock that seems to be keyless? I think not.

I'll have to remember to ask my friend this week what she did with the contents of the found drawer. I guess we already know, don't we?

"Our" Grocery Store - It's Personal

Grocery shopping is a very personal thing. Each of us has our own style of grocery shopping. My husband and I are creatures of habit and consider our local grocery store almost a club we belong to. We go often, know everyone that works there and enjoy meeting and greeting our friends as we do our shopping. We find on weekends we often go more than once a day – each!

There are many kinds of shoppers and it is amusing to study their modus operandi. There are the Hyper-Shoppers – in and out quickly, and at the other end of the spectrum the Tortoise-Shoppers – slowly but surely working their way down each and every aisle, impeding the Hyper-Shoppers. There are Price-Shoppers – they stand staring intently at the shelves in front of them insuring the per-ounce price is the very lowest and carefully matching the clipped coupons with the products in front of them.

There are the Mom-With-Kids-Shoppers. We all know them and it brings back our own memories of shopping with children. These harried young mothers trying to manage a herd of small and seeming electrified youngsters. A baby in the seat, one tugging at a hand and others running up and down the cereal aisle. Arriving at the checkout counter, they pay for their purchases, count heads and head for the SUV waiting in the parking lot.

The Regulars are seasoned professionals, going right to the milk case, the cereal aisle, the meat case where the neatly wrapped skinless chicken waits, the aisle where their laundry detergent of choice is stocked and to the register – in and out in record time.

In contrast, there are the Wanderers - new to town or on vacation, they wander aimlessly trying to locate particular items. For some odd reason the rules of the road are reversed – men will ask for directions while women won't!

Shopping is done and it is time to check out. Moving to the front of the store, I quickly scan the lines at each register to determine the one with the shortest line. Somehow, the shortest line often is the shortest because other shoppers have bailed out. The register tape has just run out, or someone who doesn't have enough money is deciding what to put back. Do you wait patiently or seek another line? It is always a dilemma.

As each shopper's choices move along the conveyor to be scanned, you can often match purchases to shoppers. An older couple, shopping together, have a small carefully selected group of groceries – orange juice, skim milk and cereal. The mother with the tugging children has virtual piles of cookies, chips, soft drinks and instant dinners.

My husband tells of standing in line one late afternoon and chatting with the owner of a local fitness center, discussing ways to stay fit, as he waited his turn to check out. Then he looked down in his basket, which was full of wine, beer and chips for a party we had planned. No fruit, vegetables or hint of healthy edibles to be seen. At that point, there is not much to say.

We always marvel at the number of people we run into when grocery shopping. There must be an axiom - the messier your hair and rougher your dress the more people you will run into. It is always an adventure – who will be around the next corner? The gentle catch-up chatter of an instant moment on the soup aisle is a special treat.

If our shopping were based on budgeting and careful purchases, we would probably make the haul to Sam's. Our preference is to shop our favorite island store, our club, and enjoy the unexpected pleasure of running into friends and associates while doing our grocery shopping.

Games People Play

When our family gets together, we inevitably play games. After a day at the beach, a game of tennis or a round of golf, we get together to share games at the kitchen table. It starts with an innocent, "How about a game?" Someone goes to the closet and pulls down a game and strange things begin to happen. Some people seem to come alive and quickly choose their seat while others involve themselves in another project or head back down the hall to their rooms. Games can be cards, Monopoly, backgammon, Trivial Pursuit or at our house the perennial favorite, Scrabble.

Not any more. Scrabble will never be the same. It has taken on a new meaning, as we have watched the most avid game player in our family "go pro". The youngest has always loved games and borders on being a hustler as he badgers people to play one game or another. He has taken his love of games and competition to a new level - he is a competitive Scrabble player, yes, you heard me right.

Organized, competitive, tournament Scrabble differs from the relaxed games we play with friends and family. Two players compete against one another - never the more social three or four. There is a twenty-three-page rule book, which governs play and includes everything from bathroom breaks to tile selection. There are more then 2,400 active tournament players. Around since 1948, Scrabble is considered a game closet basic. It was invented by an out of work architect, Alfred Mosher Butts, during the Depression and has enjoyed success ever since. The Scrabble board is a fifteen by fifteen grid. There are one hundred tiles in a set (except ours which is missing a B) which includes the two much coveted blanks.

After graduating from college and settling in North Carolina our "Scrabbler" found there was a sanctioned Scrabble Club in Winston-Salem. He now plays weekly games, has a rating and will go to the Nationals in San Diego later this year. This six-foot tall 27-year-old joins a diverse group that has little in common except their love of words. You will see men and women of all races and background competing in local, regional, national and even international tournaments. More and more young people are competing, but you still find lots of the gentle but feisty "blue hairs", as one competitor calls the more senior competitors.

We knew we were in trouble when we caught our Scrabbler with flash cards memorizing all the two and three letter words that are considered legal in sanctioned Scrabble games. In addition, he had memorized all the Q words that do not require a U (there are ten plus the plurals). He also uses new terms that are specific to competitive Scrabble. To "bingo" is to use all your letters. To try a "phony" is to try and lay down a non-existent word.

So when the family gets together and game time arrives there will be no Scrabble at our house. We prefer games that involve more luck and less skill… like tic-tac-toe.

Senior Moments

We all seem to have them - senior moments. We quickly rationalize that we are not in trouble if we are aware that we can't find something or forget something. The recognition of the occurrence insures a clear, but temporarily confused mind. I read that or heard that somewhere. But where?

Add to this, challenged vision and hearing. We dine regularly with good friends and as the menus arrive, various eyeglasses come out of purses and pockets and sometimes we actually exchange and compare our vision enhancers. Along with trouble seeing, I find that in a crowded restaurant I can barely hear. So what do I do? Smile pleasantly and nod while wondering what the other folks at the table are talking about.

My volunteer work at local assisted living facilities shows me the real face of lost memories and wandering minds. It is sad in many cases, but a certain quality of life can be enjoyed through simple pleasures like a dish of ice cream, a visit from a furry dog and a touch or pat. The same things that bring me comfort. When a weathered and ancient hand reaches to pet a visiting dog or taps a foot to music, the smile that comes demonstrates a memory reclaimed if for just a moment.

I always like the notion that our memory challenges are the result of the vast amount of information stored up top. Someone once told me to think of my brain as a huge stadium and each day more people are filling the seats making it more and more difficult to pick out one individual. This helps to visualize the challenge, but who are all those people and why are they in my stadium?

Lost items in our house are mostly keys and eyeglasses, but often it is one of the portable phones. No problem. We smugly take a cell phone, call our home number and wait for the lost phone to ring revealing its hiding place. We feel equally clever when we face a sea of cars in a parking lot and are not sure where we left ours. Smug again, we use the unlock function on the key chain, and listen for the honk or blink of a light that identifies the lost auto. Ah, we seniors are devious and find strategies to overcome our senior moments.

Haven't we all had one of those awkward moments when we cannot remember a certain name, date or fact? We know it's there. Struggle as we may we cannot bring it up. Then when we least expect it, it drops down like a candy bar in a candy machine. An 'aha' moment. It seems, often, to happen at an awkward time like sitting in church. Eager to share the lost gem - we blurt it out. People look dumbfounded at the odd piece of information you have shared, but then smile. We have all been there.

We are able to laugh at ourselves. A friend recently shared the "Senility Prayer". It asks, "God grant me the senility to forget the people I never liked anyway, the good fortune to run into the ones that I do, and the eyesight to tell the difference." Sort of tells it all, doesn't it?

Often hard on ourselves, we list our failings and frustration on losing things. Have good cheer and just remember that every school classroom at the end of each school year has a huge box of lost mittens, hats and boots. Lost items and memories are not ours exclusively. So savor those senior moments - the club is a big one and there are lots of nice people. Remember the good thing about forgetting the names of people you meet; you will keep meeting new people!

Playing Store

It is nice to be reminded once again that we live on a very special island where there are nice people doing nice things for other people. We all know that life has a way of surprising us - terrifying and unexpected surprises and wonderful, smile inducing surprises like a marriage or grandbaby. Recently a friend had a surprise that came out of left field and left her stunned.

This friend, owner of a small needlepoint and knitting shop in our little Mayberry town, moved here several years ago from Washington, DC. She followed her dream - to own a business, teach and share what she loves - needlepoint.

This brave woman and her husband walked away from good jobs in the hustle bustle of the nation's capital and moved to Fernandina Beach to enjoy a gentler pace - a place where she could hang a sign on her door that says "Open 10 ish to 4:30 ish". Owning your own business is by no means a piece of cake and it takes hard work to get past the magic two-year mark - and she did.

She not only established a loyal local clientele, but also developed a healthy mail order business for women and men who enjoy the art of using one's hands to needlepoint, knit, and crochet. Her shop is full of candy colored yards and threads and the tools of the trade - knitting needles, frames for needlepoint and the accoutrements needed to complete a project. A group meets every Friday morning in the cozy shop on Centre Street to work on their projects. They call themselves the Sexy Stitchers and are an island institution.

Everything was finally falling in place for this adventuresome couple, when out of the blue my friend's husband experienced breathing problems and knew that he needed help. They rushed him to Shands Hospital in Jacksonville, the University of Florida regional trauma center, where they knew he would get the very best care. It was touch and go. Days and weeks went by as we waited to hear that everything would be OK.

News travels fast - bad news faster than good, usually. Friends and clients knew two things. First, the couple needed to be together until things stabilized and second the shop had to stay open for the business to survive.

I quickly called a friend, an avid needlepointer and one of the "regulars". We often would run into each other while shopping for yarn or thread. "Let's play store!" I said.

We assured the owner that the "elves" could run the store and we did. We met the challenges of the impressive computerized inventory system and found ourselves helping clients with their knitting and needlepoint projects. We laughed as we found that my friend needs glasses for close-up and I need them for far away - so together we make a normally sighted person.

When we conquered a computer challenge, we gave each other a high-five. The shop continued to operate and as friends and clients came by we were reminded of the incredible depth of friendship and caring that there is in this world and especially on this island. We started a list of people who stopped to see how things were going and wanted to help.

We were able to handle the shop, so we encouraged people to pitch in when food would be needed and errands would need to be run. We all know when the going gets tough the tough start cooking. Once the patient was home and settled the casserole ladies would appear and at least for a little while food would not be a problem.

After the crisis was over, the patient came home and my friend was once again behind the counter of her beloved store. We all agreed that our gift to friends in need was also an incredible gift to ourselves. There is no better feeling than knowing you have truly helped someone.

My response when someone thanks me for a favor done: No problem, I consider it money in the bank. After all, none of us knows when we might need someone to help us run our "shop".

Vacation Resolutions

Some people make New Year's resolutions. I make vacation resolutions. Through the years when returning from a vacation that has taken me far away from my everyday routine, grind of work and home, I am committed to making some changes. Yes, I can change and return home full of resolve to make some positive changes in my busy, cluttered life.

Always high on the list is to lose weight. Unable to shed the ten (or so) pounds that came with the move to northern Florida six years ago, I continue to seek an easy, quick weight loss strategy. My closet is hung in sizes - the sizes I used to wear and those I now wear. A few special event dresses in smaller, single digit sizes hang waiting for the new slimmer me. They will probably come in and out of style several times before I have a chance to close the zipper. They continue to hang in the museum section of my closet along with my down parka, fur coat, winter boots and other dusty remnants of other times and climates.

And my house. Determined to end the clutter, I will purge great quantities of useless stuff; I tell my long-suffering husband who has heard the mantra many times before. I will pick up after myself, do laundry more often to avoid the Mt. Everest pile that impedes passage through our laundry room. Instead of the infrequent and almost military campaign approach to cleaning house, I will do a little every day and clean up after each project.

And the garage. Missing the attics and basements from other lives, my husband and I converted our garage into an air-conditioned office, storage area that is truly Fibber McGee's closet gone crazy. I call it the glacier and it seems to grow not diminish. It is hard to say goodbye, but I know in my heart when the stuff leaves the house I will not regret it. We don't even play the "one of the kids will be able to use it" game anymore - we have learned the "you gotta be kidding" look, when we offer what we consider a treasure.

Then there is the refrigerator. We share shopping and cooking at our house, and so many times items in the refrigerator remain unclaimed as each of us thinks it is part of the other's inventory. Healthy food like cottage cheese and yogurt remain untouched for months. Ice cream rarely sees the next sunset. Strange multi-colored growths on mystery items may offer the cure from some yet undiscovered disease. We always save leftovers, neatly wrapping each in aluminum foil. Weeks later the hardened relics are tossed into the wastebasket. Periodically we do a purge and fill the waste basket with salad dressing bottles with a trickle of dressing in the bottom, the open can of Coke long gone flat, stone hard English muffins, bread bags with a single piece of bread, etc.

The yard. The weeds always call. The hedge growing on one side of the house needs trimming, the decks need waterproofing, flowerbeds freshened and the lawn fertilized.

My husband willingly offers his input to my resolution list. Use your time better he counsels. I jump from work, to volunteer activities, to exercise, to projects of one sort or another. It is so hard to say "no" to all the things in my life - my multiple personalities fight for dominance. Harriet the Housekeeper always loses out. Tina the Tennis Player, on the other hand, is very successful.

Resolution lists should allow for recognition of the positive. I do have some good habits. Exercise is, indeed, a therapy for me and will not change. My tennis team is group therapy. My new yoga habit is making a positive difference in spirit as well as flexibility. Walking each morning is a wonderful shared time with husband and dogs.

Vacations away from home challenge me to think of the things that need to be done when I return. So, my lists are made as I return to ground zero. But like all resolutions, it seems hard to make those changes and in a few days after re-entry from vacation I am out the door to play tennis, pushing a mountain of laundry out of the way, but first I'll finish off last night's dessert and, I guess, I will get to the weeding tomorrow.

FALL

No More Take-Out Turkey

To me, Thanksgiving is smells and tastes. The very thought of Thanksgiving brings an instant sensory reaction. Oh, the smells…the turkey baking and filling the house with its lush perfume, the rich smell of onions crackling in a frying pan, and the teasing exotic spices that go into the stuffing and pumpkin pies. The tastes and textures vary from the cool, bumpy tart cranberry relish to the smooth pungent spiced pumpkin pie filling. The smells and tastes of Thanksgiving are like a voice of an old and much missed friend.

As I so often share, things are different here in our island home. Our Thanksgivings these days depend on our extended families' complex holiday calendars. With married kids and extended families the multiple options of whom, what, where and when have multiplied yet again. We compete with our children's spouses' families trading holidays, bartering Christmas and Thanksgiving. We are not above offering bribes – fishing, golf, tennis and, of course, the tempting warm weather.

Since moving here, we have done some experimenting with our Thanksgiving celebration and it was a mistake. Our mistake was letting someone else do the cooking. We actually ordered up the whole meal. We let them enjoy all the fun of preparations and the smells and tastes of Thanksgiving. How strange it seemed to send our head of house to pick up boxes of food instead of the traditional pilgrim hunt for the perfect bird. Instead of plucking feathers, we opened boxes of various shapes - almost like presents - each box a surprise.

Something was just not right. I felt guilty using my best china for food I did not prepare. I almost expected the holiday police would slap my hand and tell me I had broken the rules. "You can't sit in the dining room, use best china and silver, if you don't put in the time in the kitchen. You get take-out Thanksgiving then you serve it on paper plates," the holiday police would say.

This year there will be a bird roasting in the oven and pungent smells teasing a house full of family. I don't mind the kitchen time. It is part of the ritual. I even enjoy cleaning up, with help mind you. Lots of life problems can be solved as you rinse gravy off your best china plates.

Holidays always bring back memories of past celebrations. There was the Thanksgiving I cooked my very first turkey and as my young husband carved the bird in front of our guests, he held up the bag of giblets that I had not found. There were the many joyful Thanksgivings that we shared with a large family across the street. Anywhere from 12 to 24 would gather around tables throughout the house and share the wonderful food. We all had our assignments - mine were the preparation of the pies, the famous green bean casserole and sweet potatoes in orange halves.

Thanksgiving is truly a day for giving thanks - thanks for a special day where we finally take true timeouts and spend time with our families. We slow down a bit and wait to eat our big meal until mid to late afternoon. Parades blink from televisions. It is a day of anticipation. No quick meals on the run - everyone saves themselves for the big gorge. How good it is to sit over a meal with family. The meal done, we usually rationalize that a neighborhood walk will somehow offset the incredible amount of food we have just eaten. As we walk slowly in the darkening afternoon, we think about the pies still on the kitchen counter and how we might just have one more piece when we get back - after all, it is Thanksgiving.

No take-out Thanksgiving for us this year - we will go full throttle. Oh, and I forgot, the best reason to do it yourself? Leftovers!

Autumn Down in Dixie

We truly enjoy the first cool nights and the subtle changes all around as Fall comes to Amelia Island. We do not miss the abrupt changes experienced in our last home. Weather changes in the Midwest were often sudden and unpleasant, especially the days leading into winter. We have memories of snow on Halloween pumpkins and the feeling that a spell had been cast on the countryside as Indian summer faded and a thin veneer of frost covered the landscape early each morning. The shorter days seemed even more disheartening when accompanied with cold bone-chilling wind. You knew when the seasons changed.

We find season changes are so subtle in our Florida home we actually miss them. We are truly amazed as we watch the national news and see that it is snowing in another part of the country. We struggle not to gloat even after living here five years. Our move to Amelia Island has allowed an escape from the less gentle transitions of the Midwest, but we do savor a little bit of the autumn experience.

It is nice to have the windows open after being sealed in the house as we struggled to survive August's sweltering heat. Windows open, fresh air finding its way into the house and the sounds of birds and the rattle of palm leaves are welcome. The cooler dryer days make our morning walks much more pleasant and even invigorating. We find we change our clothes much less often, which means the poor old washing machine is revolving less. We don't miss the constant rumbling from the laundry room and the endless piles of clothes waiting to be folded.

It feels so good to pull on a sweater, jacket or my favorite modern invention - after white wine and hot water - fleece. This fuzzy man-made fabric feels so good, not too hot or too heavy and it is washable, always my first prerequisite. If it doesn't go in the dishwasher or washing machine, I don't want it. The bright tropical flower colors of our clothing are replaced by the more earthy autumn tones.

In our era of yard-art, the change of season is marked by a change in flags and displays, which range in sports team loyalty, seasonal exuberance, or most recently, unabashed patriotism. One could come out of a coma, walk down our street and instantly know what season it was and even what two college teams were playing that weekend.

Another sign of the season is found along Fletcher Avenue. The 'summer' people are gone and the abandoned houses display 'For Rent' signs, like dance cards, waiting for someone to sign up for next summer. Our island gets quiet in the Fall - the summer visitors are gone and we wait for the holiday visitors. We find less traffic, no waits in restaurants and parking places on Centre Street.

We are enjoying our tropical Fall and will soon watch for the next transition as the Halloween flags and pumpkins fade way and Christmas lights and Santas replace them.

Whatever Happened to Rover and Spot?

Stop and think of people you know with pets and the names that have been given to those pets. Imaginations run wild as people choose names for cats, dogs, birds and even fish. Owners, their pets, and the similarities they share from hairstyle to body shape have amused us all. Just as older couples look more and more alike as they age, it seems that pets and their owners do as well. These beloved pets all have names that somehow tell us something about them and their owners.

An instant Kodak picture pops into my mind – each morning a very sprightly, salt and pepper haired lady passes our house pulled along by her feisty and equally salt and peppered Schnauzer. True look-a-likes. An additional instant photo is my 80-something father, a Scot by heritage, and his fierce companion, a noble Scottish Terrier named Dugie. As they both take their daily walks, slowed by age and hard of hearing, they walk with the noble carriage and dignity of Scottish clansmen.

Visits to our island vet always bring smiles as I look at the family photos on the bulletin board and meet other "patients" waiting to see the doctor. A recent vet visit resulted in my meeting an elegant Dalmatian. Her name? Dotty. How perfect for a dog covered with spots.

I have met many dogs and their people through my volunteering activities in the local pet therapy program. A favorite fellow therapist is Sweet Pea, half Dachshund and half Poodle; she is a creature that the Disney people would love. Other volunteer dogs include Noble, a truly noble golden retriever, Tyler another Golden, Rip Van Winkle (he slept a lot as a puppy) a Tibetan Terrier and a feisty, at least part, Lapsa - Molly McGee. Although her heritage suggests that of a castle guard, she is much more a flirty Irish lass.

Currently we share our house with two Yorkshire Terriers. We both wonder at our dog choice, as we have both had bigger more traditional family dogs – Scottish Terriers, Corgis, German Shepherds, etc. – "real" dogs. It all began with my husband's nightly jogs and a friendship that he struck with a small Yorkshire Terrier named Maxmillian, who lives at the end of our street. We found out the name of the kennel where young Max had been purchased and made an appointment to visit. As you have surely guessed, the trip ended up in the purchase of our first Yorkshire Terrier. This small bit of dog was given the rather formal and impressive name of Oglethorpe or Ogie as he is affectionately called. Lord

From The Porch

Oglethorpe is an historic name of such note in our area that it begged to be bestowed upon on a pet. Somehow, it suits, but I suppose people and animals grow into their names.

A younger brother now joins Oglethorpe. The new puppy is a male and we wanted a name that also had a local historic ring. The name was so clearly the right one, once found there was no doubt. One of the many notorious figures in Amelia Island's history is a character named Gregor MacGregor. As Yorkshire Terriers are truly Scottish Terriers, MacGregor was the perfect name.

Our pets bring such unconditional love into our lives we do owe them very special names. The naming of pets now occupies the next generation. No grandchildren for me, I have three grand dogs. Two dogs in North Carolina, Corgis – Clyde and Alice and the most recent addition is a bulldog named Henry. "Why Henry," I asked? My oldest son replied, "Mom, he just looks like a Henry." When I met the irascible bulldog puppy, I could not help but agree that he was meant to be a Henry.

Can't Pass A Bookstore

What is it about a bookstore? We are drawn in like bees to flowers. We are blessed to have wonderful bookstores on our island, not to mention writers of all kinds. Bookstores often take on their own personalities and reflect the owners. A good friend owns a bookstore in our Victorian seaport town and meets my criteria of a special person. He had the dream and made the leap - leaving another life in another place to follow that dream and open a bookstore on Amelia Island. His love of books and dedication to promoting local writers has brought him a great following of fans, friends and customers.

He declares that he has never been happier and has never looked back. When I walk in his brightly lit bookstore at the base of Centre Strcet, I always get a greeting - a smile - and before I know it he asks, "Dickie have you read...?" If I have not, I soon find myself with the tempting new book tucked under my arm as I leave the store. Known for my facile rationalization of almost any purchase, I reflect that this indulgence is not fattening and cost less than $25.

We know the Centre Street bookstore too well. My husband and I love the library, but there is something about a brand new, never been read book that is irresistible. Books pile up on the tables beside our bed. Some are books we share, reading aloud in our efforts to avoid the squawking television. Others, on his side of the bed, are about the Civil War and history. My pile includes best sellers of all kinds, biographies and, yes, Oprah's picks.

When the piles become unmanageable, I fill grocery bags and put them in the trunk of my car. The next few weeks I become a book mobile, opening and closing the trunk many times offering my hand-me-downs to other book-a-holics in hopes of reducing my inventory. More often than not books come back the other way and the bedside piles are refreshed. The cycle never seems to end.

Forgive my use of a much-used analogy, but a bookstore is like a box of candy. Most of us when faced with a brand new box of candy will go for the ones we trust, know and love - some love the chocolate covered nuts, some the caramels. Our reading habits are like that - some always read mysteries or romances - afraid to move from our comfortable habits. Sometimes you bite into one and it is icky sweet. You bite into another and it is a pleasant surprise. The next you regret immediately, do not finish and dispose of as fast as you are able. As children, we are told to try new things, so the next time you walk into your favorite bookstore, take a deep breath and try a different piece of candy.

It's a Woman Thing

Walking into my beauty shop is like going to a very special party (women only, usually). No matter how dreary the weather or dark your mood – the bright light, clean smells and happy chatter brings one to a happier state. A good friend runs such a shop and her energy permeates her business.

There is a cozy, friendly feel as soon as you walk through the door. Soft circles of chatter bubble up around the room. The shop chatter can be of any topic – what's in the gossip magazines, who has seen a good movie or read a good book. Many times, it is the place to find out what has opened or closed on the island. As conversations develop around the shop, often a question will come up from one "station" and a voice from another "station" chimes in.

No matter what idle gossip may pass around the room, conversations always include a genuine sharing of concerns about friends, family and neighbors, who have suffered some tragedy or illness. Last fall it was my friend who needed the support as she watched her brothers die of cancer. Her "regulars" rallied around and when her birthday rolled around had an extra special birthday celebration.

I often settle down and catch up on all the magazines I love to read, but do not subscribe to – hurrying through so I finish before my turn comes. Time goes quickly and soon I settle into my chair.

There is almost a ceremony as each client settles into his or her assigned chair. The ritual begins with a discussion regarding the desired result. Arms wave, hair is tousled and a plan is adopted. The strategy may include any one or several options – a frost, a perm, a straightening, a coloring and usually a clip. The process begins – usually a trip to the sink and the wonderfully relaxing shampoo – gentle hands massage shampoo into the hair, cool water washes the soap down the drain and then back to the "chair".

Each client, damp towel on his or her shoulders, stares intently in the mirror as if the act of staring will insure a good result. Progress is made, hair is clipped, a frosting cap stretched on one's head, a multitude of small brightly hued rollers for a perm or a color rinse applied. Depending on the diagnosis and treatment there may be many trips to the sinks in the back of the shop.

Like birds preening, women look intently in the mirrors in front of them and admire their new color, fresh cut or curls. The pleasure is shared - everyone in the shop admires the freshly coifed. The bill is settled and with a fresh sense of confidence we step out into the hectic world we left not so long ago. Somehow, we expect something wonderful to happen or, perhaps, we should be challenged to make something wonderful happen.

There are gentlemen who are regulars too. Like the golf club when women invade, they are welcome. However, it is not quite the same camaraderie that the women feel. The beauty shop is a special clubhouse for a sisterhood – not that men are not welcome but you know, it is a woman thing.

It's Not Just A Woman Thing

Notoriety has its price. I must say, I have enjoyed my sense of celebrity as people mention my columns. Sure, I stay close to things that are non-controversial and talk about the island we all love – can't get in trouble, right? Who would have thought my column on going to the beauty shop would create my first backlash?

Not one, but several gentlemen have taken me to task. Clearly, the same kind of 'envelope of caring' affects their spirits as well. Is this what it means to get in touch with your feminine side? Guess men can feel a little shaggy and down in the dumps too. A sprucing and clipping may be just what the doctor ordered.

Gotta give them credit. They have found a comfort level in the traditionally feminine environs of a beauty shop, and, of course, we women are on the golf courses albeit from shorter tees. So why did they flee from the traditional bastion of male chauvinism -the striped pole barbershops?

What happened to barber shops? Where are the chatty barbers in their dark, clubby, men-only shops? When did the guys seek more pampering and a greater variety of options for their hair?

The barbershop to me brings images of Floyd in Mayberry waving his well-sharpened scissors as he clips and talks, clips and talks. My Kodak picture is of a small, dark, smoke-smelling space with sports magazines and guys hanging around talking about politics, the latest off-color joke and, of course, the sports of the moment – football, basketball, baseball or golf - depending on the season. I have memories of taking my young sons to the local barbershop for haircuts. Clearly, I was not expected to wait – just leave and come back at the appointed time.

As a small boy climbed up in the big leather chair with its chrome trim, there was no question of style or which side a part might be. The only question was how short – and in the summer it was very short. Times have surely changed as unisex salons have popped up everywhere.

So forgive me gentlemen, you are, of course, welcome anytime. You have found the comfort zone that we ladies have long enjoyed. I guess I have to admit I admire the men who join the chatter and energy that is part of the beauty shop experience and best of all you guys do look a lot better!

Soft Touch – Animals Bring Comfort

When I tell people that I volunteer doing pet therapy some immediately understand that the pets are the therapists. The visits of pets to hospitals and care facilities, has been growing across the country as people learn the simple joy that a soft furry friend can bring to a person in pain or lonely for attention and stimulation. Other people look at me with great sympathy imagining my two lively Yorkshire Terriers being analyzed and medicated by a psychiatrist. Nope, my two 6-pounders are experienced therapists.

Several years ago, I joined a friend, Sandy, who was a trained volunteer for a formalized pet therapy program in New Hampshire and who wanted to continue her volunteer work on Amelia Island. Her therapists include two tail wagging Golden Retrievers - Amber and Tyler. We contacted local care centers and assisted living facilities and offered weekly visits.

Tyler, a 10-year-old English Golden Retriever, is one of Sandy's two dogs. Tyler is blessed with the gentle, patient personality needed for pet therapy visits. Amber often stays home, a little too excitable for the visits. My two Yorkshire Terriers, Oglethorpe and MacGregor (Ogie and Mac) began to join the Friday afternoon visits. Soon others joined and included another Golden, Ramsey, and a Tibetan Terrier, Rip Van Winkle (Rip), two Corgis, Pebbles and Missy, Molly McGee, a Rescue League survivor and Sweet Pea, an irresistible cuddly combo of Dachshund and Poodle.

Clearly, our strange collection of animals is a highlight as we join a group waiting for our weekly visit. Once the dogs arrive smiles spread like lamps turned on in a dark room. Frail hands reach out to pat the soft fur. The smaller dogs jump up to settle in laps and Tyler sits with his great tail thumping the floor, baleful eyes enjoying the gentle petting. Sometimes Tyler's paw raises for handshake.

The tougher visits take us behind locked doors where the memory-impaired residents are living out their lives with little joy or distraction. When the dogs arrive, there is a transformation among the ghost-like group gathered in a small sitting area. A spark, however weak, is created as each person connects with Tyler, his small Yorkie buddies or one of the other dogs in the program. Nothing is said, a dog is deposited on a lap or held up for a pat and a door opens just a bit as a smile crosses a haunted face

The dogs are very at home and thrive on the attention they receive. As the weeks and months go by, the dogs and owners get to know the residents and anticipate their reactions to the dogs – some odd but always gentle. Visits are made to those restricted to their beds, as well, and the smaller dogs settle in quickly and it is sometimes difficult to pick them up and take them away.

Weekly visits include a stop to see a very sociable lady, who lives with her beloved poodle at one of Amelia Island's assisted living facilities. Not sure whether the visiting dogs would upset thc resident poodle the weekly volunteers did not stop at first. We later found that she very much wanted a visit. Now Sam the Poodle and his mistress welcome visitors each week .The dogs sit in a circle peacefully while Sam sits on the arm of his mistresses' large over-stuffed chair, establishing beyond a doubt that he is head-dog.

At another facility, a tiny, beautifully coifed woman looks forward to the weekly visits. After a tap on her apartment door, the dogs are wel-comed in for a slurp of water from a lovely Limoge bowl and accept the biscuits kept for their visits. As each resident is visited, the dogs sense when to come forward and, in the case of the smaller dogs, even jump in laps. There is a gentle trust between the animals and the residents of the care facilities.

We learn each week that a 'soft touch' is good medicine indeed.

Fernandina Beach Ghost Stories

Fernandina Beach has ghosts. The Halloween season brings out everyone's fascination with ghosts and ghouls. The Amelia Island Museum of History was asked by the Chamber of Commerce to add a ghost tour in the month of October to its other regularly scheduled tours of historic houses. The museum staff went to work and developed a tour featuring the more prominent ghosts in Amelia Island's history.

A good friend, who is a trained museum docent, took on the project and clearly delighted in collecting the ghost stories. The tour is based on research done through the museum and highlights some of the more notorious ghosts of the island. Many of the stories have been handed down from generation to generation or have been recounted in letters and newspaper articles.

Several houses are featured on the tour, but none is scarier than the Eppes House located on the corner of Ash and 10th Street. The house is paintless, missing many windows and in desperate need of repair but still stands proud with classic lines and elegant bow windows. The old house has a ghost - one of its former owners, Celeste Eppes. Eppes is described as a tempestuous raven-haired Creole woman with a fiery temper.

According to legend, Celeste wanted to make her husband jealous and lied about another man's inappropriate attentions. Her husband, like many gentlemen of his time, took matters in his own hands and shot and killed the named man. Unfortunately, the man was not only innocent, but also the father of six children.

In later years, Celeste died in childbirth along with her baby and is buried in the graveyard at St. Peter's Episcopal Church. Fast forward and evidently Celeste chooses to revisit her old home in the middle of the night. The current owner described the visitation in the night. It was Celeste, appearing with her signature raven hair flowing, but with a dramatic addition - a white streak. The white streak? The mark of Cane for her guilt in the death of an innocent man.

One of the last stops on the tour is the popular Palace Saloon. Even the Palace has a ghost. Charlie, an employee for more then 50 years lived in a room behind the saloon. Known as Uncle Charlie, he used to delight in making bets with customers that they could not balance a coin on the cleavage of the buxom carved figures that are still part of the elaborate mirror behind the bar. The customers predictably missed and the coins would fall to the floor. After the bar closed, Charlie would pick up his 'tips' for the evening.

After his death the tradition continued and those picking up the coins from the floor could feel Charlie's ghost close at hand. Charlie died in the room behind the saloon where he lived for many years. After his death, it is reported that the door to his room would open and close for no apparent reason.

The ghosts of Amelia Island appear to be friendly. Some are concerned about how things are arranged on a dresser and rearrange them in the night. Some open and close doors and come and go during the night. Some rock back and forth in rocking chairs protecting neighborhood pets. Some are associated with strange smells, candles in one house, and musk in another. Pets are not excluded in the island ghost stories. My friend unearthed an interesting bit of ghost trivia. Evidently, dogs can live with ghosts, but cats won't live in a haunted house.

The gentle ghosts of Amelia Island are not interested in scaring anyone, they just like to come back and visit.

So, Who's The Parent?

I recently traveled to Maryland to spend time with my father. Like so many people, I find my focus has been on parents, or in my case, a surviving parent. My 88-year-old father is a fiercely independent old Scot who now faces health challenges. Although fully capable of understanding the issues and making decisions, his hearing and eyesight are so compromised that he needs an interpreter, and sometimes an advocate.

Somewhat proficient at "med speak," thanks to WebMD, I do what I can to interpret and keep patient and medical staff at peace. Who knows, I may head to the Mid-east and further test my peacemaking skills.

My father is typical of his generation - conservative, traditional and, yes, chauvinistic. My role as daughter and his as father have been right out of central casting. He, Henry Fonda, the lovable curmudgeon of *On Golden Pond* and me Jane Fonda.

So many of us are sharing similar experiences, and wonder what our future holds. We ask the question: Is it better to have all your marbles and some infirmities, or no marbles and no knowledge of how bad off we really are? I guess I opt for marbles.

So, the roles reverse and I find myself as the one who is depended on when, for all my life, it is my father whom I have depended on. Aging can be so many things - sometimes it's sad, and sometimes it's funny. I find myself urging my father to eat his applesauce and promising ice cream. He gives me that "look" I remember so very well, and I fear that I will be sent to my room.

He may need special care, but don't mess with his razor-sharp mind and wit, and don't dare patronize him. Always a gentleman, he remains a gentleman, even in the gray-green neutral box of a room in the community hospital where he recovers from his most recent indignities.

As doctors and nurses come and go to check on his progress, he retains his humor. One white-coated visitor reviewed his chart and seemed somewhat amazed at the array of problems my father had survived. Dad seemed strangely proud, and with a glint in his eye, told the visitor, "But I've got my original knees and hips." Indeed he does. Of course, some things never change. A pretty, young nurse coming in with a smile brightens his day.

The rhythm in a hospital is irritating and frustrating to the inmates, who forget this is not a four-star hotel but a highly responsive business doing its best to take care of the patients in its care.

"Ridiculous," says my father as he relates being awakened to take a sleeping pill and getting a dinner tray at 4:30 p.m. Yes, hospital time is different from real time. Better to just recognize and accept HST, Hospital Standard Time, because it will never change.

We never learn. We fire questions at each official hospital person who enters the hospital room, asking when a patient will be released, or when the doctor will stop by. We will always get an answer, because no health professional will say, "I have no idea," which is closer to the truth. We might as well insist on an accurate weather forecast. The variables in a hospital schedule are no more predictable than the weather, but we do persist, demanding answers.

Better to think of the hospital as a ship. Once in a hospital, like setting sail, you cannot leave and are dependent on the folks in charge. Make the best of a rough sea, trust the captain and mates, and you will have a better voyage.

WINTER

Chilly Paradise

Below freezing? Frost? But we live in Florida. What is going on? Watching the island react when we have unseasonably cold weather can be amusing.

Everyone everywhere talks about the weather, but here in northern Florida, when it gets cold, weather talk can get intense. No idle chatter; we are challenged by conditions that we thought we had left behind. For those of us that come from "the North" our usual seasonal gloating is replaced by our humbled recognition that even Denver, Colorado is sometimes warmer than our Florida home. We have avoided sending our usual smarmy notes and emails to our geographically challenged families and friends.

Strategies and reactions can be many and varied. People experience flashbacks to lives in colder, grimmer climates where they have lived or spent time. Local people remember the time it snowed on the island.

There are some good things about the challenges of colder weather. We trade our marsh side porch for the living room and its fireplace. For us, the colder temperatures mean nightly fires crackling as we watch television or read aloud to each other. Home and hearth are comforting and bring good feelings. Normally not a dependable or regular cook, I go domestic. Comfort food - popcorn, pots of chili, corn bread, cocoa and hot cereal emerge from the usually dormant kitchen. My husband seems to enjoy his temporary reprieve from nightly barbecue duty.

The landscape has a brittle, lifeless look. Strange shapes loom in front of houses as people try to protect their treasured bushes and shrubs from the nightly frosts. Sheets and bedding of all description cover the endangered plants. They look like small, plump ghosts huddled close to the house waiting to be uncovered with the first sunny day. Watering systems, which have evidently not heard the nightly frost warnings, cover yards with icy coatings that glow in the early morning sunlight.

Dress changes. Gone are the soft pastels, shorts and cotton sweaters. Layers of darker, richer colors and even earmuffs and woolen hats are the norm. Our usual tennis group, eager to be outside and to get needed exercise, vow to continue our usual matches. We meet at our scheduled time and chuckle as we admire our strange and varied costumes that have been designed to deal with the cooler temperatures. For many it means raiding our "Northern" closets and dressing like small children bundled against the cold. In the end, we are glad we made the effort and enjoy the games; shedding layers as the sun warms us.

So what to do when the weather turns cold? Celebrate the cozy. Read the book that has been waiting for your undivided attention. Attack the refrigerator in need of a cleaning. Organize the piles of family photos in albums. Remember to feed the birds and offer them water – they too get stressed when Florida plays a trick and turns cold. Change and challenge are good. The cold spells are temporary and are soon replaced by the more typical and balmier temperatures. Our unusual cold weather will be a memory and weather talk will be about how hot and humid it is!

Gift Guilt

It has begun – a headache that will not go away – my annual malaise – Gift Guilt Syndrome. Every year as the holidays approach, I think there has to be another way. The commercial chaos swirling around the holidays truly offends me. Advertising all around reminds us how many days are left…left until we realize we have forgotten someone or wish we had done more or even, in some cases, less.

Moth to flame, I am seduced by the never ending tugging at my holiday buying dollars. Each touching family scene, pictures painted of rosy-cheeked perfectly dressed children, smiling faces, endless good food and piles of elaborately wrapped gifts that stare back at me from magazines and newspapers feed my neurosis. Turn the television on and one is faced with baskets of puppies, and beautiful horses pulling sleighs through snowy pollution free snow and all with endless classic Christmas carols blaring. Who said Christmas had to be loud? Like Pavlov's poor dog, I search for my purse sensing I must grab it and buy a present for someone.

Gift giving guilt. What is it? Do we do it to ourselves or are we hapless victims sucked in by a hard pushing retail conspiracy? Taken to extreme, Neiman Marcus comes up with the ultimate Christmas gift each year – always outrageous and expensive. No hot air balloons or fish tanks only slightly smaller than a small ocean for our family. We are more a Target kind of clan.

As my young sons grew up, I dreamed of a Walton Christmas – a rustic cabin somewhere in a wooded, not too cold, but cold enough for snow, kind of place. Christmas would be a snowy night; a fresh cut Christmas tree, hand-made ornaments, fire in the fireplace, a turkey in the oven and a loving family. But best of all – no gift guilt. Why? Because everyone would share a handmade gift. Something baked or a special piece of time to share a talent or task. We would make something good to eat, write a special story or poem, promise to help with someone else's household jobs, give a pass for the movies, teach a game or skill like knitting or playing chess. What a nice fantasy.

We did actually achieve a simpler gift exchange one holiday season long ago. When the children were very young and not yet corrupted by the shameless and endless commercials painting pictures of happy families exchanging many and costly gifts, we did give gifts that were made of thoughtfulness and caring. The special gifts included cards and pictures crafted out of odd and assorted household items. Still smelling of school glue and shedding glitter, macaroni and buttons, a Charlie Brown Christmas tree remains a favorite in my memory. We gave each other "promises" written on scraps of paper to be claimed in the coming year. One promise – a shared ice cream cone at a future date (from Mom). Another promise – leaf raking with a cheerful attitude (from son).

The simpler holiday gift exchange went by the wayside, as I was not strong enough to work each year to "keep it simple". Now, as each holiday rolls around, I get the guilt headache. Recently an opportunity presented itself. A family gathering brought all children and significant others in one place. Being a creative and not to mention brave soul, I presented the assembled family group the dilemma – make the holidays guilt free – at least regarding gift exchange. So what did they think? No big expensive gifts - maybe edible or readable gifts instead?

A democratic process ensued. I proposed: "Let's exchange books, we all love to read and can pass our books to others." A grumble passed around the table – some liked it, but more did not. Next idea? One daughter-in-law suggested adopting a strategy much like her large family has done. Each family member draws a name and buys one gift. A positive mumble erupted and questions began to pop out. One gift to purchase – one nice one instead of a pile of mixed value – yes the group decided this is good.

How much to spend? How do you know what your person might want? The democratic process progressed, names were drawn and dollar limit set. A palpable sigh of relief passed among us. We will see if it works. Another holiday season. Another chance.

Recipe Book of Memories

Personal gifts are the best gifts, both for the giver and the receiver. Each holiday season I hope to find something that I can make and give that is personal. This may date back to childhood when our family tradition was to bake and make things to share with friends, neighbors and those people who were constants in our lives. The holidays were the time we thanked people who did things for us – as small children we would rush from the house with a plate of homemade cookies for the garbage man, the milkman and the postman. The home baked gifts came from the oven and the heart – what gift giving should be about.

The Christmas after my mother died, I indulged my creative self in a project that became part of the longer than expected grieving and healing. After her death, one of the more bittersweet moments came as I began to look through her recipe box, the one I remembered so well. Sitting on the floor, and looking at each stained card, yellow with age, brought memories flooding back.

Different handwritings and credits would remind me where the treasured recipe had originated. Mother's friends had shared many of the recipes, most of them now gone, and from lives long since lived. An idea blossomed, I would sort and edit and reproduce those that held the strongest and most treasured memories. Once duplicated they would be shared with family and Mother's friends. She would have been so flattered and pleased.

So many of the treasured recipes are tied to holiday memories – sugared nuts, gingerbread men and the butter cookies in fanciful shapes. Making the cookies meant being together – busy in the kitchen – mixing, baking, decorating and finally packaging. We would mix our various cooking creations and put them in baskets or special holiday plates, wrap them in cellophane and tie a bright ribbon around.

The old recipes bring such vivid memories. Especially the Christmas cookies. I can smell the cookies baking, feel the sticky frosting on my fingers and hear giggles as family members created some very original Christmas cookies. Another memory that is not quite as pleasant – the stomach aches from cookie dough overdose. The Christmas cookie recipe is the one I made as a girl with my mother and sister and in turn made with my young sons, who now are making them to give and share.

Some recipes were instant finalists. Aunt Martha's Company Casserole, the traditional Green Bean Casserole, Ultimate Chocolate Brownies, Christmas Butter Cookies and on and on. Other recipes joined the classics and soon I had a selection of recipes ranging from nibbles to desserts and everything in between. Recipes selected, I began the process of copying the final selections and listening to my printer as it clicked and clacked turning out half-sheet pages. The next step – holes punched and bright ribbon binding the book together.

The process of going through the old recipe box, holding my mother's favorites recipe cards in my hand, caught me short and brought a tear, but the end result became a gift to me. The gift is from my mother and in a way, her mother (some of the recipes were hers). Sharing the cookbook with each of my children, my mother's friends and mine, was the best holiday gift of all.

Being Santa Claus

Ever wonder what it might be like to be on the other side of a red velvet suit and a snowy white beard? Well... been there. It is an unexpected Christmas gift to those lucky enough to be inside the classic crimson suit of Christmas. Each holiday season, activities press on us from every direction, but one we will not give up is the donning of the velvet. My husband and I welcome our time getting in character, and, at least for a little while, being the most loved characters of all time.

We were asked if we would help at some holiday events and dress as the venerable Mr. and Mrs. Claus. The first time we dressed in our costumes of velvet and fur it took on the sense of a sacred ceremony - the royal order of Santa Claus. I watched as my everyday husband was transformed before my very eyes. Admittedly, he comes with a built in twinkle in his eye, so once you add a snowy white beard and wire spectacles - voila Santa. No mop hat and tiny glasses for this Mrs. Claus. I wear a short-skirted velvet dress, a Santa hat and carry a bag of small toys for the youngsters we meet.

Being Santa is to feel the generosity and true glee that the season brings. As we go out to meet our public, would children see through our masquerade? Once on the other side, snug in our crimson velvet, we find ourselves taking on the persona of the jolly couple. We field questions and bring smiles with the ease of seasoned Santas. That is not to say the Claus' don't have to stay on their toes. As one child sat on Santa's knee, a cell phone went off in Mrs. Claus' bag. Santa, in a panic, looked at his wife who deftly explained it was just the elves checking in. The child was impressed and so was Santa.

Whatever discomfort we feel disappears as the first children approach us with true wonder and awe in their eyes. Reactions vary. Some children will stand back and watch Santa and then slowly circle closer and finally settle on his knee. Some will simply howl in terror and attach themselves, as if glued, to the nearest parent. As each child stops to talk to Santa, somehow Santa knows just what to say. It must be something built into the suit of velvet and fur.

Some of the very best reactions come from the grown up children we meet. Even the most jaded adult will smile and greet Santa and his perky wife. Some have smart remarks, but all in good humor.

Everyone seems to remember the Christmas they "found out" and how many more years they pretended to believe. Well, we become believers each time we become the gentle old couple - yes, it's a gift once a year to be Mr. and Mrs. Claus.

Santa Brought A Hot Tub

We have talked about it and talked about it, but it took Santa to make it happen. Our hot tub sits on our screened porch standing ready to bubble away our cares and woes and comfort our achy bodies.

The topic usually came up after a long day in the yard, a tough tennis match or lengthy golf outing. Wouldn't it feel good to slip into some hot steamy water? We listened as friends bought their hot tubs and worked through the deliberations that were required. Where would it go? What color? How big? Who would take care of it?

My Santa announced at Thanksgiving that as much as he would like to surprise me, he would need my input. This was to be the Christmas of the hot tub. We have been married long enough that he knows some surprises are good, but not many. Knowing that I might have some opinion, he let the tub out of the bag and suggested we check out the options.

Only those who have gone through the process know that hot tub shopping is like shopping for a car. As we approached the first show-room, I was forewarned that the options were many and to stay focused. The salesman crossed the room, and remembering my husband, led us to the "Ecstasy" (they have names likes cars) and began to describe the therapeutic benefits. I looked around the room at the various models in shades of blues and greens. Taking a deep breath, I announced what I considered our criteria. Not too big (our porch is small), not hard to take care of and with jets that hit the part of my back and neck that so often beg for some kind of relief.

We were invited to try them on. We did not go so far as donning bathing suits and slipping into the swirling waters of the showroom models, but we did get in to test the molded tubs and their various options for seating. It so boggled our minds that we left the showroom babbling at each other about the pros and cons of various models. Were we really ready to take on the spa thing? A spa? The models we had just looked at were certainly more than hot tubs with the prices they begged - at some point they become spas - around $2,500.

As we discussed options, we remembered friends that had purchased a less overwhelming option... a soft-sided hot tub. They were enthusiastic about their tub and how easy it was to maintain and use. To make a long story short, Santa tracked down the local dealer, and Thanksgiving weekend an oversized kiddy pool sat at the far end of the porch waiting for customers.

The customers came. Hot tubs offer a kind of forced intimacy, which is so welcome in this day and age. No television, no computer, no newspapers or other distractions - just the company of the person joining you for extended conversation while the warm water swirls and the jets gently massage your back.

Thanks Santa. At the end of the day, our "tub time" is special.

Holiday Hangover

Admit it. We all make New Year's Resolutions whether we fess up or not. The Christmas tree is on the curb and the holiday clutter is tucked away in boxes waiting for next year. One resolution I did keep one year was to do a better job of packing Christmas up and putting it away.

In the frenzy of holiday shopping, I found specially designed boxes that hold Christmas ornaments and one box in particular that stores lights. I smugly purchased them and savored the opportunity to bring order out of chaos after our seasonal celebrations.

Typically, once presents are open, Christmas dinner consumed and family members are long gone, my strongest instinct is get all the endless clutter tucked away. The tree project is usually left to me. I brought out my specially designed storage boxes and began the task of dismantling it. Strange how men disappear when the Christmas tree is being taken down. There I was, the tree and me. Determined to be organized in the process, I first packed our potpourri of odd ornaments each in their separate compartments in their clever new box.

Each year I resolve that I will sort ornaments from my children's childhood and give them to each now. They have their own homes with basements and attics - let them put them away. A bit daunting and a lot sad, each year I put it off until the next year.

Then the lights. Personally, I think tree lights are a guy thing. But with my special "light" box awaiting, I turned to the lights. With the full confidence of a person trying a new system, I wound the lights on the cardboard forms designed to keep them orderly. Once wound on the form, the form fits in slots that separate strands one from the other. I almost gloat as I think of next year and skipping the frustrating ceremony of plugging in lights and untangling strings.

The tree decorations neatly packed away, I begin the hunt for endless Christmas doo-dads tucked on tables and on walls, windows and doors around the house. I never find them all on the first round and weeks later will find a Santa or snowman in some forgotten corner.

Each year there is a new decoration. One year, a few days before Christmas, busy in the kitchen, I thought I heard someone at the door.

The dogs sounded an alarm, but when I got to the front door, I saw no one. I turned to pull the door behind me, heard a rattle and something bright red caught my eye. A cheery wooden snowman smiled back at me, a clever hanging decoration on the doorknob. A friend who charms those close to her with thoughtful handmade gifts had hung the snowman on the door with our name in white lettering that looked like icing on a gingerbread cookie. That is what Christmas is about - surprises and thoughtfulness.

New Year's Grinch

I am a New Year's Grinch. The thought of New Year's Eve makes me grumble. One day, one hour, one minute, one second. Why focus on one tick of the clock? The hype paints a picture of confetti, champagne, tuxedos, and nostalgic music — all in great, extravagant quantity. But New Year's celebrations cause my mind to go in reverse - my racing thoughts play time machine and, sadly, remember rough times, lost relationships and missed opportunities. This is not the usual me. I am the queen of half-full, not half-empty. I blame the champagne that does very, very strange things to an already overly creative mind. The millennium turn and that particular New Year's challenged me.

One New Year's I will never forget - New Year's 2000. Yup, it was going to be a big one and it seemed appropriate to somehow put another spin on the event. We chose to avoid the mega galas and be with close and dear people. As we anticipated the big day and evening it occurred to us that the sunrise on the new millennium was much more exciting than a clock ticking down the seconds of the old year. After meeting friends for dinner at a favorite restaurant, we each left to pursue our private plans for the midnight moment. For us it was a spot on the beach to watch the bright and colorful Ritz-Carlton fireworks, and then home to bed.

But the real and remembered celebration came for us several hours later. Just prior to dawn, we packed a champagne breakfast, grabbed our wee Yorkshire terrier and headed again for the beach to watch the dawn of a new century or, for those purists, the dawn of an almost new century.

We arrived at the agreed upon spot to an almost Halloween-like experience - dark figures moving on the beach past the remnants of a lifeguard chair that had been part of a bonfire. Like a cult meeting at the edge of the sea, our friends slowly made their way over the dunes and joined us as the first bits of light nibbled at the horizon. It was eerie and quiet - partly the drama of the moment and partly sleep deprivation.

The sunrise on Amelia Island's eastern edge was spectacular. We were treated to a warm, still morning, and the ocean was as calm as any inland lake. As the sun slowly floated upward, its wattage increased, bathing us in a rosy, golden light, which was reflected in the glassy ocean. Each moment brought yet another subtle change in color and hue.

One of our group had a new digital camera and captured our millennium moment. They rushed home to send their sunrise photo to their children in Colorado, before they experienced their own special mountain sunrise. We toasted each other, the sun and the new century, and headed quietly back through the dunes to a slowed down kind of day.

Later a quick check of my email revealed the sunrise photos taken that morning on the beach. I quickly sent them to friends and family. My first digital moment. Somehow appropriate for a dawn of a new century.

Cumberland Island Anniversary Dinner

We celebrated our wedding anniversary in style. We celebrated over dinner like many couples do, but this dinner was unique in many wonderful ways. We went to the Greyfield Inn on Cumberland Island. The ads promoting a chance to take a boat to the romantic inn on an island reached only by water tempted us. Our special occasion was the catalyst that took us across the inky black water that separates Amelia Island from Cumberland Island, Georgia, the next island north, one dark December evening.

At 5:00 PM, we parked our car at the Fernandina Beach harbor and looked for the Miss Lucy, the boat that would take us to dinner. Climbing aboard, we settled on a bench and huddled together. As we left the dock and looked back at the sleepy little town of Fernandina Beach, it became smaller and smaller and soon looked like a string of Christmas lights laid along the horizon. The Miss Lucy is a working boat, a water taxi of sorts, and we shared our 45-minute ride with many who live and work on the island as well as a few other dinner guests.

Arriving at the Greyfield Inn dock, we were greeted by inn staff. We disembarked to find a big van waiting at the end of the dock. Chock full, the van covered the short distance to the inn and we spilled out in front of the impressive and welcoming Greyfield Inn. It continues, as it has for more than a hundred years, to provide hospitality to visitors to her island. We climbed the handsome stairway that leads to the sweeping porch that extends across the front of the sparkling white 1901 mansion. Greyfield was built as a home for Lucy and Thomas Carnegie's daughter, Margaret Ricketson. In the 1960s Margaret's daughter, Lucy Ferguson and her family opened the home as an inn.

From the moment you walk in the front door into the foyer, with its stairways going downstairs to the dining rooms and upstairs to the guest bedrooms, you are enveloped in a sense of warmth and gracious hospitality that echoes a slower paced time. We took a short tour and stopped in my favorite room, the centrally located lower level, cozy house kitchen, which is open and welcoming during and between meals. Guests staying at the inn are invited to raid the refrigerator for tasty leftovers or pick up picnic baskets packed to their specifications. The baskets may be taken to the beautiful 13 mile beach to the South end and the ruins of Dungeness, the original Carnegie mansion, or to the North end and the African Baptist church and site of the Kennedy/Bissette wedding. Adventure opportunities abound on Cumberland Island, now a National Seashore protected by the National Park Service.

Back upstairs and with drinks in our hands, we entered a wonderful salon with a large fireplace, a comforting crackling fire, dark, rich wood walls and antiques that are more about comfort and history than formality. A shabby-chicness makes you immediately comfortable.

The faces that look back at you from the photos and portraits around the room are welcoming. Clearly, they have tales to tell about the exciting days of hunting the island's wild pigs, harvesting oysters and walking the beach. They appear to welcome us this cool wintry night.

Dominating the room is a much-photographed portrait of "Miss Lucy", who spent much of her life on the island she loved. She looks back at us, beautiful and exotic with a scarlet scarf tied around her head and reminding us that we were there at her pleasure.

We shared conversations with others - a couple from New York City who had been coming to the inn for more then 18 years, another couple who amazingly live two doors down from us and a young couple from Ponte Vedra who had just gotten engaged.

We were called to dinner and joined some 40 other diners downstairs at elegant tables, where we enjoyed a three-course meal beautifully prepared and served. We sat at one end of a large dining table that sat ten people. We savored the soup course, main course of pork and fresh vegetables and finished with a custard dessert with a scattering of fresh fruit.

The dinner was over too soon, but before we had to catch our boat back, we joined other guests in the salon where after dinner drinks were served. One of the young waiters treated us to a sample of his talent. He read several poems he had written and answered questions about his work. Guests offered comments and compliments. What a contrast to our usual dining in the real world where fellow diners hardly make eye contact let alone speak. We all savored our special experience, and if for just one evening, a slower pace and the gentility of times long gone.

All too soon, we were called to catch our boat ride home. Momentarily wishing we could climb the stairs to one of the cozy rooms above, we instead left to catch the boat back to Amelia Island vowing to savor shared meals and friendly conversation.

Destination Our House

We have just finished an incredible spring of revolving doors. Our little house on the marsh has been fully booked for the last eight weeks. I am often reminded of the clever ads that Holiday Inn runs on television. The thankless young man, still living with his parents, demanding all the service and amenities of a hotel. A feisty grandmother, also living at home, cackles. After one more demand, the sharp-tongued mother snaps back at her son, "What do you think this is - a Holiday Inn?"

From The Porch

Don't get me wrong, we love company, but there are funny moments when your house becomes an 'open' one. After years of living in the heart of the Midwest with its hot, hot summers and cold, cold winters, I was not prepared for my life in Florida and the open invitation that living here implies. For some reason visitors to our Iowa home were mainly family and rarely in February, March or April. Our Florida home is clearly a preferred destination.

We all experience it. Set your calendar – first of February. The phone rings and the reservations start rolling in. We have had a particularly busy spring, as have many of our island friends. We share stories of our unexpected challenges and pleasant surprises.

My first morning instinct is to blindly head for the kitchen and the pre-programmed coffee pot with it's hot inviting brew. Always being the first up in my house, it never fails to surprise me to find a fully dressed, chipper guest sitting at my kitchen table enjoying a cup of coffee. I quickly look down at my wrinkled nightgown or my oversized T-shirt and wonder how strange my "bed hair" must look. Mumbling as I grab my cup of coffee, I retreat to my bedroom to accelerate my morning routine.

One delightful bonus of our many guests is the visits to places you always plan to go to but somehow never do. This spring brought a long overdue trip to Jacksonville and the Cummer Art Museum. We visited the museum with friends from Chicago, who were thrilled at the Cummer's riverside spring blooms. An unanticipated surprise - an orchid show right next door at the Women's Club.

We try and please our different guests and accommodate them in ways to make their visits the best possible. Our refrigerator in the garage is full of cold beer, wine and a variety of soft drinks ready for the challenge. We do get stumped occasionally – grapefruit juice? We are not always prepared for martini drinkers, but innovate quickly.

Our two guestrooms – the "blue room" and the "brown room" stand ready – brochures and tourist magazines are available and a big basket of fresh towels in each room.

Spoiled pets, expanded waistlines and neglected yard work are small sacrifices against the simple joy of friendship shared. As we show off our beloved island, we are reminded of all the wonderful things that first brought us to Northern Florida. The natural beauty of the beaches and live oak trees, the wide variety of wonderful places to eat, our unique Fernandina Beach shops on Centre Street and on and on. We never tire of our set island tour that often ends with a cold drink on our porch overlooking a marsh sunset.